THE VALUE OF KINDNESS

The Story of Elizabeth Fry

VALUE COMMUNICATIONS, INC.
PUBLISHERS
LA JOLLA, CALIFORNIA

THE VALUE OF KINDNESS

The Story of
Elizabeth Fry

BY SPENCER JOHNSON, M.D.

Second Edition
Manufactured in the United States of America
For information write to: Value Tales, P.O. Box 1012
La Jolla, CA 92038

Library of Congress Cataloging in Publication Data

Johnson, Spencer.
    The value of kindness.

    First ed. published in 1975 under title: The ValueTale of
Elizabeth Fry.
    SUMMARY: Discusses the work of the English woman
whose pioneering efforts in improving the lot of prisoners
were based on the premise that prisoners' behavior would
improve if they were treated more kindly.
    1.   Fry, Elizabeth Gurney, 1780-1845—Juvenile
literature.   2.   Prisoners and prisons—Great
Britain—Juvenile literature. [1.   Fry, Elizabeth Gurney,
1780-1845.   2.   Prisoners and prisons—Great
Britain.   3.   Kindness]   I.   Pileggi, Steve.   II.   Title
HV8978.F7J63   1976   365'.92'4 [B] [92]   76-55339
ISBN 0-916392-09-0

This tale is about a person who was very kind,
Elizabeth Fry. The story that follows is based on
events in her life. More historical facts about
Elizabeth Fry can be found on page 61.

Once upon a time...
there was a girl named Elizabeth who lived in a great
house in England. She slept in a soft bed and she wore
pretty clothes. She ate fine food and, on sunny days, she
played in the garden with her brothers and sisters.

She should have been very happy, but she wasn't.

"I like being kind to people," she said, "because it makes people happy."

"I wish I could go out and be kind to those people whom no one else thinks about."

There were days when Elizabeth was sad. It was on one of these days that a butterfly came flitting into her garden. She pretended that the butterfly was talking to her.

"Don't be so sad, pretty lady," the butterfly said. "I will help you. I will be your best friend."

Although Elizabeth knew that she had made up the talking butterfly, it was fun to think of having a butterfly as her friend.

"Why are you sad, Elizabeth?" the butterfly asked.

"I am sad because I am not being kind enough to people," said Elizabeth. "I live in a great house. I sleep in a soft bed and I wear pretty clothes. Everyone is good to me. But I know that many people have no one to care for them or to be kind to them. That makes me unhappy."

"I can see how that might trouble you," the butterfly said. "I just flew over Newgate Prison, and it troubled *me* to see the way the women prisoners there have to live."

"Oh, dear!" said Elizabeth.

The butterfly rested on a flower. "I know what it's like to be in prison," it sighed. "I used to be a caterpillar, and I lived in a cocoon. I couldn't move around and I couldn't get out. It was like being in a kind of prison."

"How dreadful!" said Elizabeth. But then she brightened up. "I know!" she said. "I'll go to see the women at Newgate Prison. Perhaps I can help them."

And she ran into the great house where she lived.

She knew that the women in prison didn't have pretty clothes. "I'll change my dress," she said. "I don't want to remind them that they don't have pretty clothes. That would just make them more unhappy."

So she put on a simple gray dress and covered her head with a plain white hat.

"I'll go with you," offered the butterfly, "but not if I have to change my clothes."

Elizabeth laughed. Everyone knew that a butterfly couldn't change its clothes.

Then Elizabeth told her father she wanted to visit the women at Newgate Prison.

"No, Elizabeth," he said. "The women at Newgate are criminals. They have been locked up because they did bad things. You are much too young to go among criminals. It's too dangerous. You might be hurt.

"But never mind," said her father. "You may be young now, but you'll be older soon enough. Why not go and cheer up the people in the hospital now, and later you can visit Newgate."

At first she was sad, but then she thought "That's a fine idea!"

Off she went to the hospital, and she had a smile and a kind word for everyone. The sick people were happy to see Elizabeth. They were glad that she cared enough to come and visit them.

Elizabeth was busy and happy, and time passed quickly. She did get older, and she got married, so she had a new last name. It was Fry.

One day Elizabeth Fry decided she was ready to visit the women at Newgate Prison.

"Be careful," warned the butterfly. "Some of the women were bad people even *before* they went into prison. But it is so terrible inside the prison that *now* most of them have become even meaner. The women are very cruel to one another. They might even be cruel to you."

Elizabeth Fry wasn't afraid at first, but when she got inside the prison she was very upset.

"It's frightful!" she cried. "So filthy! And the air is so bad that I can hardly breathe. What a terrible way for anyone to live."

It was indeed terrible. The women inside the prison had become lazy and dirty. They were uncombed and dressed in rags. They shouted and quarreled with one another.

Why?

Because they had nothing better to do. Besides, no one cared what they did. No one had ever taught them to be kind to one another.

"Oh, no!" said Elizabeth Fry, when two of the women began to fight. They tore at each other like wounded animals. They swore and bit and kicked each other.

"Please, please stop!" cried Elizabeth Fry.

23

The women did stop fighting. They stared at Elizabeth Fry.

"Here's a fine lady come to make fun of us," said one.

"Let's tear her pretty clothes," said another.

"We can black her pretty eyes," said a third.

"But I didn't come to make fun of you!" said
Elizabeth quickly. "I want to help you."

"Perhaps we should leave," said the butterfly.

"You can leave if you want to," said Elizabeth. "I'm going to stay." And she tried to smile at the angry women.

"I say," said one of the women, "there's something different about this fine lady. She doesn't have on pretty clothes. She isn't wearing any feathers or flowers that we can pull off."

"What will we do to her?" asked another woman.

"The prisoners are closing in on Elizabeth Fry," called one of the guards. "I'm afraid they're going to kill her."

By now Elizabeth was afraid, too. The prisoners had crowded so close to her that the guards could see only the top of her hat. "I won't show that I'm afraid," said Elizabeth to herself. "I'll stand still.

"If only I could make them believe that I'm here to be kind to them!" said Elizabeth Fry.

"Perhaps you can," whispered the butterfly. "Look over there at that poor, sick child."

Elizabeth looked. And then she did something that surprised everyone—everyone except the butterfly.

Elizabeth moved away from the angry women and hurried to the little child, who was lying on the cold floor. She picked the child up in her arms.

"Friends," she said to the prisoners, "many of you are mothers. I, too, am a mother. I am distressed for your children. Is there not something we can do for these innocent little ones? Do you want them to grow up to become real prisoners themselves? Are they to learn to be thieves and worse?"

Suddenly the women stopped shouting and threatening. They began to cry soft, happy tears.

"She *is* kind," they said. "She *did* come to help us."

"No one outside the prison has ever worried about our children, or about us before," said one of them, and she brought a chair for Elizabeth Fry to sit on.

Then all of the women who had children brought
them to see Elizabeth Fry.

"We must do something about these children,"
Elizabeth told them.

"Perhaps it would help to start a school for the children here in the prison."

The children had never met a grownup who came and paid attention to them and worried about them. They weren't used to it, but they liked it. They smiled timid little smiles.

"They look happy," thought the butterfly. "At least, they look happier than they did a few minutes ago."

Elizabeth Fry did start a school for the children of the women prisoners at Newgate. She taught them reading and spelling and sewing.

Most of the mothers couldn't read or spell. They would peep in through the door of the schoolroom and think, "We wish we could go to school, too."

At last some of the women went to Elizabeth Fry.
"Can we please have a school too?" they begged.

"I'm not sure," said Elizabeth. "The officials who run
the prison might not like it. But it can't do any harm
to ask them, can it?"

Elizabeth Fry invited the prison authorities to her home, and she asked them about the school.

"If we could make the prison a nicer place," she said, "and if we could teach the women something useful, they might live better lives once they were out of prison."

"It won't work," said the authorities. "However, we'll let you try it just to show you that you are wrong to be kind to prisoners."

So Elizabeth Fry started a school for the women prisoners of Newgate.

"When you can read and write," she told them, "you will be more likely to succeed and not return to prison."

"I wish that I could read and write," thought the butterfly. But it couldn't. Butterflies simply do not read and write.

Butterflies don't sew or knit, either, and Elizabeth Fry taught the women sewing and knitting.

"When you learn to make things," she said, "you can support yourselves from your *own* work. Then, when you get out of prison, you won't have to beg or steal."

"Wonderful!" thought the women. They were very happy making colorful quilts in their prison school.

"I'll take your quilts and sell them for you," said Elizabeth Fry. "Then I'll give you the money and you can buy some little things for yourselves."

"You're very kind, Elizabeth Fry," the prisoners said. "Thank you."

For many of the women, the money they got for the quilts was the first they had ever honestly earned. They were able to use it to buy sugar and tea at a little store in the prison. They felt so proud of their efforts.

"I'm very happy," said one of them. "I've never been so happy before."

Then one day the authorities came around to see how things were going in the prison.

"What's happened?" they cried. "Look over there! How clean everything is. And look at those women. They're bright and happy and pretty."

The women had cleaned the prison up, you see. And they had cleaned themselves up. The prison looked like a busy little shop or a friendly home. The women were not fighting. In fact, they were helping each other.

The prison officials were so impressed that they told the people in the village about the change in the prison.

"Look at it!" they said. "See how nice it is now. It's a much better place since good, kind Elizabeth Fry came here to help the prisoners."

Later they called a meeting.

"We have men prisoners at Newgate, too," said one of the officials. "Perhaps we can help them, the way you have helped the women."

"You should," said Elizabeth Fry. "You can help them just by being kinder to them. It seems that when you're kind to someone, that person is more apt to be kind to you. Wouldn't it be wonderful if we could teach all the people in prison to be better, kinder people?"

"We'll try!" shouted the officials. "We'll begin by opening schools in all of our prisons!"

They did open schools, and it worked. When the prisoners knew that someone cared about them, and when they learned to do something useful, they weren't nearly so likely to get into trouble again.

Soon Elizabeth Fry was getting letters from all over Great Britain. She got so many letters that her daughters had to help her with the mail.

"Here's a special one, Mother," cried one of the girls one day. "It has a red seal on it." Whom do you think it could be from?

Elizabeth Fry was very happy when she opened that letter. It was an invitation from the House of Commons to come and tell the members how they should treat people in British prisons. It was the only time a woman, other than a queen, had been asked to speak to the government.

"Can I go with you?" asked the butterfly.

"Of course," said Elizabeth. So she and the butterfly went to the House of Commons.

"The answer is very simple," she told the distinguished men. "Prisons should be schools of reform—places where people who have been bad can learn how to be good. You will never teach people to be good by being bad to them—by beating or starving or humiliating them."

She went on, "The answer is to be kind, to help people, to care about making them happier. When people are happy, they will be good."

"She's right, you know," said the members of the House of Commons.

"I'm so proud of you Elizabeth," whispered the butterfly.

After that, Elizabeth Fry was invited to go to the Continent of Europe to talk with kings and queens and heads of state. They all wanted to know how to make their prisons better.

She rode in a carriage to see them.

Elizabeth Fry told the kings and queens of Europe that people, even prisoners, are more likely to be good if you are kind to them.

As Elizabeth spoke, she felt very happy. She knew
how *good* it feels when you show kindness towards someone.

Perhaps, like Elizabeth Fry, you might like to think about how good you feel when you are kind.

Of course, you may decide to bring kindness into your own life in a very different way, indeed. But whatever you decide to do, let's hope it is something that will make you a happier person . . .

Just like our kind friend Elizabeth Fry.

The End

ELIZABETH FRY
1780-1845

Elizabeth Fry did more than any other person of her time to bring about prison reform, which began in England and spread to much of the Continent of Europe.

She was born Elizabeth Gurney in 1780. Her father was a British banker, and he was so successful that the English took to referring to wealthy people as,"rich as the Gurneys." The family were Quakers, but not members of the strict group who were called "Plain Quakers." But when Elizabeth was seventeen, she did become a Plain Quaker, dressed in plain clothes and gave up all personal adornments.

She married Joseph Fry, who was also a Quaker, and became Elizabeth Fry.

She first learned about the conditions in Newgate Prison in 1813. The prison was located in one of the oldest and worst parts of London. Four hundred women lived there, crowded into four little rooms. Fifty children had been imprisoned with their mothers. They were clothed in filthy rags. There were no beds, no bedding, no toilet, no heat, no ventilation and no light.

Elizabeth Fry and her Quaker friends began their work at Newgate by bringing warm clothes and education to the prison. Elizabeth also brought hope, and she spoke of the need for the women to reform themselves. Not only did she talk to the women, but she talked to prison officials and lawmakers, encouraging them to be more considerate of the prisoners.

Because the behavior of the prisoners did improve dramatically when they were treated more kindly, Elizabeth Fry's ideas spread throughout England. Also, rulers in France, Holland, Denmark and Prussia welcomed her advice. The Emperor of Russia followed her suggestions for a new prison in St. Petersburg. Her plans worked so well that he exclaimed, "She's one of the wonders of the world!"

Joseph Fry, Elizabeth's husband, did not always approve of her activities. However, he had promised never to interfere with her work, and he kept his word. With this support from her husband, Elizabeth Fry was able to enjoy her marriage and also to concentrate on her work and do it well. She had eleven children, the last of whom was born in 1822, on the same day as the first of her twenty-five grandchildren.

Before her death in 1845, Elizabeth Fry had led reforms in many areas. She founded societies to look after women prisoners after they were discharged. She worked to change the law itself, for at that time the law declared that a man, woman or child might be hanged for housebreaking, shoplifting or small theft.

One of her reports, made to the King of France, ended with words which have lived to this day: "When thee builds a prison, thee had better build with the thought ever in thy mind that thee and thy children may occupy the cells."

The ValueTale Series